COOKING WITH

TINNED
FISH

weldon**owen**

CONTENTS

INTRODUCTION

TRAVELING TO FISHING COMMUNITIES ALL OVER THE WORLD inspired me to give the fishermen and their wonderful stories their place on cookbook shelves. Their sustainably caught fish is the foundation of the recipes in this book. By supporting sustainable fish, we give endangered fish populations the opportunity to recover. So let's get to work with sustainable fish—the fisherman with nets and rods, the cook with pots and pans.

To make sure the fish lover is able to enjoy both preserved and fresh fish in the future, many fisheries will have to start operating differently from how they are now. And by buying only sustainable and fresh fish, the consumer can make an important contribution to that endeavor.

If there's one thing I've learned during my travels, it's the fact that we can make a big impact on sustainability by making ethical choices about tinned fish. After all, a lot of wild fish ends up in a tin. These fish are accessible and affordable to many, even if you're on a budget, and with tinned fish you can easily prepare tasty and nutritious meals.

We often don't know where fish comes from and how it was caught. The lack of good information prevents consumers from making the right choices to suit their lifestyle. Because tins have labels, it is easy for the manufacturer to inform the consumer about what fish are in the tin, how they were caught and what happened to them between the sea and the tin. Transparency makes all the difference. You need to know the stories behind the product in order to love the product. That's why you won't just find unexpected recipes in this book, you'll also get to know the fishermen and manufacturers. They made the conscious decision to fish with the environment in mind or use sustainable fish in their products. By opting for sustainable products, consumers can in turn influence fishing methods and fish populations.

More and more tinned fish manufacturers are taking responsibility by adding certification labels from organizations such as the MSC, the Marine Stewardship Council, and the Monterey Bay Aquarium Seafood Watch. The MSC continually verifies fisheries' compliance with protocols, for example, minimizing the bycatch of dolphins caught in tuna nets. The certification label assures the consumer that the fish they've bought has come from fisheries operating under sustainable fishing guidelines.

In addition to the fishing method, flavor is of course very important in the product. Mass production and anonymity often negatively impact flavor and quality. I've found that doesn't have to be the case. That's why I founded Fish Tales, offering the tastiest tinned fish, smoked or fresh, caught by environmentally responsible fishermen. They view the seas and oceans as the source of all life. Their fish has no artificial flavor. Try it, taste the difference and judge for yourself.

Tinned fish is surprisingly versatile in the kitchen. We took the task of creating sumptuous dishes with tinned fish as a challenge. The results may surprise you. We selected fifty of the best recipes from an impressive collection. This book offers you the best of both worlds: fresh produce combined with tinned tuna, anchovies, mussels, salmon, mackerel, sardines, crab, cockles, and herring.

BART VAN OLPHEN, AUGUST 2014

LOOKING BACK

THE LIFE OF OUR TINNED FISH STARTS, oddly enough, with glass. At the end of the eighteenth century, the industrial revolution led to a sharp rise in the population of the industrialized nations; and more people called for more food. Fridges hadn't been invented yet, and transportation of fresh produce was slow. Preserving methods such as drying, smoking, pickling, curing and conserving in fat or sugar offered little relief and were too expensive on a large scale. Cheaply and safely preserved food was supposed to be the solution for the growing need for food. Even Napoleon Bonaparte faced the troubles of perishable foods, which threatened his ambitions. Hungry soldiers are hardly the ideal force to help you win battles, and in 1795 the French government offered a money prize to whoever could make preserved, nutritious food for a soldier's ration.

At the time, French confectioner Nicolas Appert was experimenting with food. Appert had years of experience in the techniques of making syrups and confectionery, and he began heating jars of food in water up to 212°F/100°C, then cooling them down. Once he had perfected the technique, he achieved the desired outcome: he was able to successfully preserve meat, vegetables and fruit by the technique now known as sterilization. Although preserving fruit by heating it is a technique that had been around long before Appert, he was the first to research the effects of airtight seals and applying high temperatures to food. Appert eventually supplied the navy, which intended to use his preserved fruit to prevent crews from contracting scurvy. When his efforts proved successful, the navy informed the French government, which awarded Appert the prize money in 1810. Appert's jars enabled the troops to charge into battle well fed, and his conserving method survived Napoleon Bonaparte. The confectioner could easily be seen as a food scientist *avant la lettre* and the founder of convenience food. Louis Pasteur would later improve on Appert's technique, turning down the heat by about thirty degrees. Pasteurization killed enough harmful bacteria and retained more flavor.

The French government insisted Nicolas Appert should publish his research. *L'Art de conserver, pendant plusieurs années, toutes les substances animals et végétables* is probably one of the first books on preserving food that found its way into many households around the world. In Britain, the book found its way to Pierre Durand, a Frenchman who anglicized his name to Peter Durand. He held a patent for conserving food in glass and tin cans. Appert nudged Durand in the right direction, but Durand didn't pursue the business further and sold his patent cheaply to Donkin, Hall and Gamble. Bryan Donkin recognized the potential of conserving food in tin cans. Tins were lighter than glass, didn't break and were easier to manufacture. Again the navy, this time the Britsh navy, served as the testing ground. The rest is history: the British tin came, saw and conquered. The French have one more addition to the history of tinned food. Grimod de la Reynière, a friend of Nicolas Appert, wrote about the sardines of Nantes conserved in butter, oil and vinegar, before Donkin went full steam ahead with his tins. The efforts of Nicolas Appert and later Louis Pasteur form the basis of the food industry as we now know it. Even now the availability of affordable conserved food means not having to go hungry for millions of people around the world.

FROM TINSMITH TO AUTOCLAVE

ONCE UPON A TIME, TINS WERE SUPER SEXY. The only tins getting any respect these days are the tin cans on wheels. Once it became available, preservation techniques such as freezing rapidly overtook the tin. However, it's time the tin gets some more recognition. The modern tin is strong, hygienic and easily recyclable. The use of corrosion-resistant, light aluminium and thinner metal increase the recycling options and lower the carbon footprint in production and transport. The materials are pliable and easy to open: great for whether you are in the kitchen or trekking through the Andes. The tin's contents are portioned so there is less waste. Most people use the contents in one go, but if you do have any left over, you can remove it from the tin and keep it in a covered container in the fridge a couple of days or even freeze it. A tin always offers a readily available stash of nutritious and reliable food.

It wasn't always like that. Making tins used to be manual craft. For many, tinsmith was a highly regarded profession. Tinsmiths made all sorts of items by hand from tin-plated sheet iron—such as biscuit and cocoa tins. To increase production, the manufacture of tins for foods containing liquids was mechanized. It didn't all work perfectly from the start: the moisture and acid-rich foods caused rust in the tins. The manufacturers were also not able to mechanically seal the tins and opted for bendable, poisonous lead to solder the tins shut. In turn, this made them difficult to open—a chisel was often the opener of choice! However, through trial and error, manufacturers kept improving tin cans. The arrival of the tin opener also increased their popularity, although the first tin opener wasn't exactly fit for domestic use. It was basically a modified bayonet that made it easier for soldiers to get to their baked beans. Thinner metal made way for the more useful tool with a cutting wheel.

Galvanization with zinc countered rust corrosion, and creasing and welding techniques made lead unnecessary. The acidity continued to be a challenge, and for a long time, the metals continued to leave a distinct tin flavor in the food. Eventually the invention of a plastic coating made this a problem of the past.

The pressure cooker, a seventeenth-century invention by the Frenchman Denis Papin, made it truly possible to deliver tinned food safely, as high-pressure steam cooked the food more quickly. Two hundred years later, the Brit Charles Chamberland invented the autoclave, a further development of Papin's pan. The autoclave is used to sterilize food under high pressure and at temperatures reaching 212°F/100°C and higher, doing away with the need for preservatives. Most manufacturers add at least some salt, so they can sterilize more quickly or at lower temperatures. The once infamous, gas-bloated tin of rotten foods is now—even past the expiration date—a thing of the past. Only less stable ingredients like crab are still assisted by stabilizing agents in the tin.

THE SEASON IN A TIN

"TIN THE FISH ON THE DAY OF CATCH BEFORE SUNSET." That's a saying popular with many tinned food manufacturers. They prefer to process fresh goods in season, and for fish this means tinning as soon as possible after catching. Tests have proven that the nutritional value of modern tinned food comes close to that of fresh. Storing product also costs money. Reducing the heating-process time also reduces the energy bill. Tinning doesn't guarantee good flavor though; flavor depends on the production methods and the quality of the original product used. Like all other foods, tinned fish is all about picking the right producers.

This might come as a surprise to many, but tinned fish is a very seasonal product. Not only that, but it also comes from well-managed and healthy stocks. The fisheries catch the fish only when the fish is in the right shape for consumption, and none of the fish is lost in production. All these aspects are important in maintaining both the quality of the product, the protection of the environment and the sustainability of the fish stocks.

The better producers will provide clear information on the contents of the tin and where it's from. Tinned fish is available from large-scale companies who use multiple canneries that tin other foods in addition to fish. On the other end of the spectrum are many smaller, often family-run businesses, especially in areas of Europe such as Brittany, the Spanish Basque Country, northern Portugal, Denmark and northern Germany. They tin fish from day catches and use high-quality oil or carefully selected sauces. These products are found in the aisles under their own names or as part of, for example, the Fish Tales line. It is definitely worth reading the label first before making a decision on which tinned fish to buy.

A TALE ABOUT PORTUGUESE FISHING COMMUNITIES

THE FISHING VILLAGE MATOSINHOS IN PORTO once housed more than two hundred *fábricas de conservas*, which mainly processed Portugal's famous sardines. New food safety regulations and a demand for higher quality meant the end for many of these factories. Because they held onto their traditional ways for too long, they weren't able to modernize. A bit farther north in the fishing village Póvoa de Varzim, fishing factories met their demise. The factories were only running when sardines populated the Portuguese coast—from April to October —but employees would continue to be paid throughout the rest of the year. These businesses valued their employees highly because they would be nowhere without the women—who comprised the bulk of the workforce—who carried out the manual labor. This model, however, was not profitable enough to sustain.

The family running A Poveira factories realized they needed a change of approach. They were selling their sardines under the well-known name Minerva and were able to find investors who believed in the future of supplying high-quality tinned fish. Changing their methods would lead to an even higher quality. They closed down their old factories and opened a new cannery in Póvoa de Varzim, where, in addition to sardines, they are now able to process different fish, which means employees can work throughout the year.

A Poveira's ultra-modern factory might look less appealing than an old-fashioned version, but its production of the highest-quality tinned fish is what matters. Skilled women are still at the heart of the company. Rather than going into mass production, which often leads to loss of flavor in the final product, A Poveira combines modern techniques with the skilled work of dedicated craftswomen to achieve even better-tasting fish.

Many manufacturers fill their tins with raw fish, which are then heated to 212°F/100°C after sealing—cooking and sterilizing the fish at the same time. This approach generally leads to loss of flavor. A Poveira first steams their sardines and mackerel, after which skilled laborers carefully clean and pack the fish into the tins, sometimes with herbs and spices. The tins are then filled with good-quality olive oil, water or a sauce, depending on the product. Finally, the tins are sealed mechanically and briefly sterilized.

A Poveira uses tastings to convince their visitors that their approach works. Premium brand Minerva's Portuguese sardines have a distinctly pure flavor. The Fish Tales sardines are made by the same people. The flesh on the removed bone still has that characteristic rose-tinted color of fresh sardines. The mackerel's strong flavor and meaty bite also impress.

A WOMAN'S STRONGHOLD

"TU É EU, NÓS DOIS" IS TATTOOED on many a woman's skin: You and me, always together. The man at sea, the woman on land, always connected. The men run the seas, but women rule the dockside. They take the crates of fish from the men, sort the fish and clean them in the factories. Men have earned their place in the fish trade though. You can recognize their warehouses by the pictures of famous soccer teams like FC Porto and Sporting Portugal.

DESIGNER TINNED FISH

A Poveira couldn't have timed the new development better. High-quality tinned fish is gaining in popularity—and not just in Portugal. Young entrepreneurs like José Ricardo Silva are capitalizing on this trend.

Silva opened a pop-up store in Porto around Christmas 2013. It was a success, and Silva decided to open a permanent shop: Central Conserveira da Invicta. The sardines are supplied by A Poveira and Silva designs the tins himself. You won't find tins as colorful and vibrant as these anywhere else. The Porto town center is home to a couple of speciality stores, like A Favorita do Bolhão, that stock a wide range of tins.

And here are some more tips to remember when you're on vacation visiting the wonderful city of Lisbon. Go to the Conserveira de Lisboa in the old city center. You'll find a shop with a 1930s-style interior design where the walls are lined with tins. The proprietors produce their own tinned fish and create sauces to accompany the sardines. Café Sol e Pesca in Lisbon simply has tinned fish with bread and a delightful wine on the menu—a perfect combination. Mercearia das Flores in Porto also serves tinned fish, with the local bread delicacy, broa, made from corn flour. If you want to go upmarket, visit Can the Can in Lisbon, where the chef offers innovative dishes using fresh as well as tinned fish.

COOKING WITH TINNED FISH

THIS BOOK OFFERS THE BEST OF TWO WORLDS by combining tinned fish with fresh produce. Tinned fish is very versatile, especially when you're aware of this rule of thumb: fish in water is best used in cold dishes, and fish in oil can be used in both hot and cold dishes. This is because fish in water is drier than fish in oil and heat will further dry the fish. Lean fish, like tuna in water, go well with fatty products like mayonnaise and cheese. However, don't be restricted by these rules. If you let your imagination run wild, you'll doubtless create delicious recipes of your own, especially if you use seasonings like lemon, tomato and black and white pepper, which can really elevate tinned fish.

The quality of the oil used with tinned fish can vary wildly. If you've got a good product and the oil smells and tastes good, you can use the oil from the tin in your dishes. If not, just drain the oil and use your own.

Cockles, crab and mussels are well suited for use in both cold and warm dishes. Remember to add them to a dish like a soup or pasta just before serving only to heat through, otherwise the shellfish can overcook and lose their flavor.

SPECIES	Albacore tuna and skipjack tuna
BINOMIAL NAMES	*Thunnus alalunga* and *Katsuwonus pelamis*
FISHING METHODS	Pole and line-caught
MSC CERTIFIED	Predominantly the skipjack fishery in the Maldives, also the American Albacore Fishing Association in the United States (for more information on the MSC, see page 6)
TINNED OPTIONS	Tuna in water, tuna in sunflower oil, tuna in olive oil

ONLY WHEN WE COEXIST WITH NATURE, WILL THE CATCH BE BOUNTIFUL.

TUNA

IF YOU WANT TUNA, BUY A TIN OF SKIPJACK, THE STRIPED TUNA. The skipjack is less threatened in its territories, and dolphins don't populate the same areas. The albacore, the white tuna, known in Spain as *bonito del norte*, can also be a sensible choice, provided it is supplied by a fishery known to use sustainable sources.

The other species of tuna are in worse shape. Most supermarkets now reject tins of yellowfin tuna, and the survival of the famous Atlantic bluefin is seriously threatened, so it is best left alone. Certainly in Western countries, you are increasingly likely only to find skipjack or albacore on the shelves, as more and more supermarkets exclude other types of tuna. If the tin shows the blue MSC eco-label, you know you have certified sustainable fish in your hand. Also look for keywords such as: Albacore, skipjack, troll-caught and pole-and-line-caught.

What is in the tin? Precooked tuna. Albacore is lighter in color and flavor compared with skipjack. The belly, the expensive and fatty *ventresca*, is mostly sold in flat tins and jars. The other parts of the tuna, including the trimmings, are all packaged in round tins. Whether you use larger or smaller chunks is up to you, but a large chunk of tuna, from a steak, represents the highest quality. Of lower quality is a tin with large chunks pressed together, while the lowest-quality tinned fish consists of many smaller pieces. The quality can vary from good to rather mediocre, but fortunately an increasing number of manufacturers now indicate whether their tin contains steak or chunks, which gives you some options. Finding good tuna is a matter of trying multiple tins by different brands.

The tastiest and best-quality skipjack is found in the Indian Ocean, near the Maldives, the string of 26 atolls and 1,200 islands with their countless stunning sandy beaches. Tourism is a good source of income for the locals, but the real sharks among them choose a life on the seas. They can always fall back on peddling drinks and snacks. Week after week, Ali Mohamed and his band of fishermen cast their rods into the ocean. This line-catching method almost completely eliminates the bycatch of vulnerable sea creatures. Tuna live in large schools, which makes rod fishing economically viable. At night, Ali shines his floodlights, attracting small fish like moths to a flame. The fish are pulled aboard and stored in saltwater tanks. The next day they serve as live bait for the tuna.

ALI'S AND JACK'S GRACEFUL, CONTROLLED LINE FISHING

The fishermen aren't fazed by the swell of the ocean. They continue to cast their lines relentlessly, as if their lives depended on it. A mist of spray shrouds the ship, which distracts the tuna so they can't see the ship. One by one, the fishermen haul tuna onto the ship until they run out of bait, then they pack up for the day, even if there's plenty of tuna left in the sea. Overfishing is beneficial neither to the fish nor to the fishermen. It is now time to go back to Mandhoo, the fishing village on Laamu Atoll, and rest on the pearly white sand of the coconut palm-shaded Mandhoo Beach.

Line fishing appears to be the obvious method of countering overfishing, as fishing with nets ensures the catch of large numbers of fish in one go. However, in reality it is less straightforward. Line fishing of endangered fish stocks can be just as harmful to a species. "Only when we coexist with nature will the catch be bountiful," says Ali Mohamed. A truly sustainable fishery relates to more than just the fishing method. Especially in areas where the local population has few

alternative means of making a living, fisheries can contribute to supporting local communities. The fishermen in the Maldives are a good example of this. In the company Horizon, they control the supply chain, from the catch to the tin. Everyone involved in the fishery earns a decent income as an independent entrepreneur. This approach attracts interested buyers who, together with the International Pole and Line Foundation, financially support local initiatives like the fishers school. When you buy MSC-certified tuna, you can rest assured you're supporting environmentally responsible fisheries. However, do note that only 8 percent of the world's tuna catch complies with these conditions.

On the other side of the planet, on the West Coast of the United States, tuna fishermen do their bit as well. They have renounced the infamous drift nets, and Jack Webster and his colleagues angle with rod and line for albacore, the white tuna, on the southern coast of California. Timing is of the essence when fishing for albacore. When the hook hits the water, the tuna swims toward the hook at 25–30 miles/40–50 kilometers an hour. The tuna bites and will dive back down immediately. At the precise moment the fish bites, the angler has to forcefully pull the fish out of the water. If the fisherman is just a split second too late, the tuna will drag the rod down into the sea. This approach results in healthy tuna stocks and has the added advantage that dolphins will rarely be tempted to bite baited hooks. As soon as the fish is caught, it is placed in brine at 7°F/-14°C. This cooling technique ensures that the quality of the fish meat is maintained. When you see the boats in the harbor filled with tuna, it's hard to believe each fish was caught individually. In 2008, this "one man, one hook, one fish" attitude resulted in an MSC certification for the world's first sustainable tuna fishery.

TUNA SPAGHETTI WITH CAPERS AND OLIVES

MAIN COURSE
SERVES 4

olive oil
2 tsp tomato paste
2 red bell peppers,
    seeded and diced
3 tins of tuna in olive oil,
    (3½ oz/100 g each),
    drained and flaked
1½ cups/12 fl oz/350 ml
    tomato paste
2 tsp capers, rinsed

¼ cup/1½ oz/45 g chopped
    black olives
1 bay leaf
1 lb/16 oz/500 g spaghetti
3½ oz/100 g Parmesan cheese,
    freshly shaved
salt and freshly ground
    black pepper

- Heat a dash of olive oil in a large frying pan. Add 2 tsp tomato paste and fry over medium heat for 1 minute.
- Add the peppers and fry until softened.
- Add the tuna and stir to blend the ingredients.
- Add 1½ cups/12 fl oz/350 ml tomato paste, the capers, olives and bay leaf and stir, then leave the sauce to heat through over low heat, stirring occasionally.
- Meanwhile, bring a pot of water to a boil with a pinch of salt.
- Add the spaghetti and cook until al dente according to the instructions on the package.
- Drain the spaghetti, then spoon it into bowls.
- Turn the heat up under the sauce, stir well and season to taste with black pepper. Spoon on top of the spaghetti.
- Serve with Parmesan cheese in a separate bowl.

CHUNKY TUNA MESS

SNACK/STARTER
SERVES 4

This recipe is an adaptation of a traditional Flemish tuna salad called *smos-tuna*—and *smos* means "to mess or fiddle with,"—so this title seemed appropriate for this tasty little salad, which has no measurements. Just mess around with it however you like, as long as you flake the tuna into large chunks.

mayonnaise
crème fraîche
3 tins of tuna in water
    (3½ oz/100 g each),
    drained and flaked into
    large pieces
1 carrot, grated

1 jar of pickled onions
1 jar of gherkins in vinegar,
    cut into chunks
4 slices of bread, toasted
handful of watercress
salt and freshly ground
    black pepper

- Combine equal quantities of mayonnaise and crème fraîche and season with salt and pepper.
- Mix in chunks of tuna, the grated carrot, and pickled onions and gherkins to taste.
- Spoon onto the toast and garnish generously with watercress.

VEAL MEDALLION AND TUNA PASTE SANDWICH

generous ¾ cup/7 fl oz/200 ml
   chicken stock
4 veal medallions, ½ in/1 cm
   thick
2 tins of tuna in water
   (3½ oz/100 g each),
   drained
2 eggs, hard-boiled
2 anchovies
3 tbsp mayonnaise

1 tbsp olive oil
1 tsp lemon juice
4¾ oz/135 g arugula leaves
1 baguette, cut into 4 pieces and
   split in half horizontally
2 ripe tomatoes, sliced
2 tbsp capers
freshly ground white pepper
1 bunch of radishes, washed

- Bring the stock to a boil.
- Add the veal medallions and simmer in the stock for 4 minutes. The meat should still be pink.
- Remove the veal from the stock. You can use the stock as the base for a tasty soup.
- To make the tuna paste, use a food processor or blender to blend 2 tablespoons of the stock with the tuna, eggs, anchovies, mayonnaise, olive oil and lemon juice until completely smooth.
- Divide the arugula among the 4 baguettes. Place the veal medallions on the arugula. Generously spread tuna paste on the medallions.
- Garnish with slices of tomato and sprinkle with capers, then finish with a grinding of white pepper.
- Serve the sandwiches with the radishes.

TUNA AND TOMATO PASTE MILLE-FEUILLE

SNACK/STARTER
SERVES 4

2 tins of tuna in water
    (3½ oz/100 g each),
    drained and flaked
3 tbsp mayonnaise
2 tbsp crème fraîche
4 sun-dried tomatoes, drained
    (if from a jar) and
    thinly sliced

6 sprigs of rosemary, leaves
    finely chopped
9 oz/250 g rye crispbreads
1 red onion, thinly sliced
4 ripe tomatoes, sliced
salt and freshly ground
    white pepper

- Using an immersion blender, mix together the tuna, mayonnaise, crème fraîche and sun-dried tomatoes.
- Season with rosemary, salt and pepper.
- Spread the paste on the crispbreads.
- Place the sliced red onion and tomato slices on the tuna paste.
- Layer the crispbreads to make the mille-feuille.

TUNA AIOLI, BACON AND AVOCADO PITA

SNACK/STARTER
SERVES 4

olive oil

9 oz/250 g cherry tomatoes, halved

3½ oz/100 g sliced bacon

4 pita breads

2 ripe avocados

juice of 1 lemon

6 garlic cloves

4 slices of bread, crusts removed, then toasted

½ cup/4 fl oz/125 ml mayonnaise

2 tins of tuna in water (3½ oz/100 g each), drained

1 green onion, chopped

coarse sea salt and freshly ground white and black pepper

- Heat a dash of oil and fry the tomatoes over medium-high heat for a couple of minutes.
- Remove from the pan, sprinkle with salt and white pepper and set aside.
- Heat a frying pan and fry the bacon until crispy. Leave to drain on paper towels.
- Lightly toast the pita breads in a toaster or under the broiler, then split in half horizontally.
- Halve the avocados and remove the pits. Scoop out the flesh with a spoon, cut into slices and drizzle with lemon juice.
- Using a mortar and pestle, crush the garlic cloves with a pinch each of sea salt and white pepper, 1 tbsp olive oil and a slice of toasted bread. Fold in the mayonnaise to make aioli.
- Purée the tuna in a food processor or with an immersion blender.
- Mix the aioli with the tuna.
- Spread the tuna aioli on the inside of one half of the pitas, then top with the bacon, tomatoes and avocado. Sprinkle with green onion and finish with some freshly ground black pepper. Top with the other half of the pita breads.

TACOS WITH FRESH TUNA SALAD

MAIN COURSE
SERVES 4

¼ cup/2 fl oz/60 ml
    mayonnaise
2 tbsp full-fat yogurt
1 tbsp ketchup
2 tbsp olive oil
1 red onion, thinly sliced
3 small gherkins in vinegar,
    drained and finely chopped
1 tbsp capers

2 tbsp lemon juice
1 tbsp freshly ground black
    pepper
3 tins of tuna in water
    (3½ oz/100 g each),
    drained and flaked
4 taco shells
5½ oz/150 g mixed greens

- Preheat the oven to 375°F/190°C.
- Mix together the mayonnaise, yogurt, ketchup and olive oil thoroughly.
- Add the onion, gherkins, capers, lemon juice and black pepper and stir them together well.
- Mix the tuna flakes into the dressing.
- Heat the taco shells in the oven for 3 minutes.
- Let the tacos cool a bit, fill with the tuna and serve with the salad greens.

TUNA PASTE AND ROASTED PEPPER WRAP

STARTER
SERVES 4

2 red bell peppers, halved
  and seeded
2 tins of tuna in water
  (3½ oz/100 g each),
  drained and flaked
½ cup/4 oz/120 g Indian chile
  relish
3 tbsp mayonnaise
1 tbsp olive oil

4 tsp chopped thyme leaves
4 small tortillas
2 red onions, thinly sliced
  into rings
2 tbsp capers, drained
  and rinsed
salt and freshly ground
  black pepper

- Preheat the grill. Put the peppers on the grill, skin side down, and grill until the skin blisters and turns black.
- Put the peppers in a plastic container or bag, seal and leave to cool.
- Once cooled, the skin will come loose. Remove the skin and cut the flesh into thin strips. Set aside.
- Preheat the oven to 350°F/180°C.
- Using a food processor or immersion blender, blend together the tuna, chile relish, mayonnaise, olive oil, 2 tsp of the thyme leaves, salt and pepper.
- Place the tortillas in the oven for a few minutes, until lightly browned.
- Spread the tuna paste on the tortillas and top with the sliced onions, peppers and capers. Sprinkle the remaining thyme leaves over the top and season with pepper. Roll up and enjoy.

WHITE TUNA AND GREEN HERB COUSCOUS SALAD

STARTER
SERVES 4

scant 1½ cups/9 oz/250 g
   couscous
chicken stock
olive oil
1 large red or green bell pepper,
   seeded and cut into strips
3 tins of tuna in water
   (3½ oz/100 g each),
   drained and flaked

1 large red onion, sliced into rings
a few sprigs of dill
a few sprigs of basil
a few sprigs of flat-leaf parsley
a few chives, cut into long pieces
coarse sea salt and freshly ground
   white pepper

- Cook the couscous in the chicken stock according to the package directions, then leave to cool. Stir with a fork to loosen the grains, then drizzle with olive oil and season with salt and pepper to taste. Stir again.
- Put the pepper pieces onto four plates or bowls and spoon the couscous over the top. Add the tuna flakes.
- Garnish with the red onion, dill, basil, parsley and chives.
- Drizzle some olive oil over the salad to finish.

SPECIES   Anchovy

BINOMIAL NAME   *Engraulis anchoita*

FISHING METHOD   Pelagic trawling

MSC CERTIFIED   Argentine Anchovy Fishery (Mar del Plata)
                   (for more information on the MSC, see
                   page 6)

TINNED OPTION   Fillets in oil

SOAKING ANCHOVIES IN MILK, WINE OR WATER GREATLY ENHANCES THE CULINARY POSSIBILITIES OF THE HUMBLE FISH.

ANCHOVIES

ANCHOVIES ARE RELATED TO HERRING, so they belong to the family of oily fish. Oily fish are perfect for fermenting in brine, which tenderizes the meat, and the anchovy is no exception, but it is time-consuming. Tinning anchovies in salt and oil is a much quicker technique, but it won't tenderize the fish—in fact it toughens it slightly. Tinned anchovies are not sterilized, because applied heat will only result in fish pulp. The quality of the products can differ, but at least a tin of anchovies is not expensive. Buy a couple and see if you agree: tinned anchovies can surprise you.

The preserving method limits the capabilities of tinned anchovies in the kitchen. They are mostly used to add a kick of flavor to dishes. Soaking anchovies in milk, wine or water greatly enhances the culinary possibilities of the humble fish. You can also mellow the saltiness with some butter. Oil offers the adventurous cook the chance to add surprising touches as well, following in the footsteps of the ancient Romans who used the fish sauce *garum* to spice up their dishes. Fish sauce is still widely used in Asian cuisine. In Thai it's called *nam pla*, in Vietnamese *nuoc nam* and in Chinese *yu lu*. All of them use anchovy as the main ingredient. Southern European countries like Italy also make their own very expensive fish sauce from anchovies: *colatura*.

THE ARGENTINES GET IT COMPLETELY

Forty years ago, Mariano's family's fishery used to fish around Argentina's large seaside resort of Mar del Plata with a fleet of small boats. It was hard making a living that way, so the family decided to sell off their boats and invested in a couple of larger vessels. This enabled them to sail farther out to sea and fish for anchovies. During that time, Mariano experienced the consequences of overfishing. Something had to change. Mariano chose restrained fishing and had the MSC scrutinize his methods. He got the go-ahead: his is the world's first MSC-certified anchovy fishery. One hopes this milestone will inspire the numerous fisheries along the South American coast, because Latin American fisheries play a big part in the global fish trade. Their approach can make all the difference.

True fish lovers leave tinned fish like anchovies and sardines to mature in order to reach a more complex flavor. Turning the cans keeps the fish from drying out. To accommodate the fish lover, some French producers state the season in which the fish were caught. The area where the anchovies were caught, the name of the boat and the name of the fisherman can also be available: useful information for consumers who want to know what they're buying.

Only a few manufacturers offer MSC-certified anchovies from Argentine waters. Others would rather not spend the money or, more often, don't see a profit in fish with the blue eco-label. However, they will guarantee the anchovies are caught with ring nets, which eliminates most bycatch. That sounds good, but only the MSC eco-label gives the consumer traceable certainty regarding the fishing method.

RIB-EYE STEAK WITH ANCHOVY BUTTER

MAIN COURSE
SERVES 4

2 heads garlic, cloves separated
    and peeled
2 tins of anchovy fillets in olive
    oil (1¾ oz/50 g each),
    drained
3½ oz/100 g butter, softened

1 shallot, finely chopped
1 lemon
4 rib-eye steaks (7 oz/200 g
    each), at room temperature
salt and freshly ground black
    pepper

- Preheat the oven to 400°F/200°C.
- Wrap the garlic cloves in aluminum foil and place in the oven.
- After 20 minutes, check on the garlic by squeezing one of the cloves. If it's completely soft, take the foil packet out of the oven.
- Using a fork, mash the anchovies into the butter.
- Mix the shallot with a squeeze of lemon juice into the anchovy butter, cover and set aside.
- Trim any excess fat off the meat and cut the fat into cubes.
- Heat a frying pan and fry the cubes over medium heat until golden brown. Remove from the pan and set aside.
- Season the meat with salt and pepper.
- Fry the meat for a few minutes on each side over high heat until browned and cooked to your liking. Remove the meat from the pan, cover and let rest for at least 5 minutes before slicing.
- Serve the steak with the anchovy butter, the roasted garlic, the fried cubes and an extra sprinkling of black pepper.

CITRUS ANCHOVIES AND GRILLED ZUCCHINI

STARTER
SERVES 4

juice of 1 lemon, strained
juice of 1 orange, strained
generous ¾ cup/7 fl oz/200 ml
    balsamic vinegar
a few sprigs of basil
heaping ⅓cup/1¾ oz/50 g
    pine nuts
1 tin of anchovy fillets in olive
    oil (1¾ oz/50 g), drained

milk (optional)
peanut oil
1 zucchini
a little olive oil
a few sprigs of thyme,
    leaves separated

- Put the lemon and orange juice, balsamic vinegar and basil sprigs in a pan and boil until reduced by one-third.
- Remove from the heat, take out the basil sprigs and leave to cool, then chill in the fridge.
- Heat a frying pan and toast the pine nuts until golden brown.
- Desalt the anchovies by soaking in lukewarm water or milk for a few minutes, if you like. Drain and pat dry.
- Remove the vinegar mixture from the fridge and beat in a few drops of peanut oil.
- Cut the zucchini crosswise into 3 pieces, then cut the pieces lengthwise into slices about 1 inch/2.5 cm thick. Brush with olive oil and grill on both sides until browned.
- Place the grilled zucchini slices on a large plate. Sprinkle the balsamic dressing over the vegetables and serve with the anchovies, pine nuts and thyme leaves.

COLD SPANISH SOUP WITH ANCHOVIES

STARTER
SERVES 4

15 ripe tomatoes, chopped
a few pieces of stale baguette
6 eggs
6 garlic cloves
olive oil

cayenne pepper
red wine vinegar
butter
16–20 anchovy fillets
salt

- Using an immersion blender, purée the tomatoes, bread, 2 of the eggs and the garlic cloves with a generous dash of olive oil, a pinch of salt, and cayenne pepper and a splash of red wine vinegar until you have a smooth soup. Chill in the fridge.
- To poach the remaining eggs, bring a pan of water to a boil. Grease some plastic wrap and place in a cup. Break one egg into the cup.
- Carefully lift out the plastic wrap with the egg and tie a knot to enclose the egg. Repeat with the other 3 eggs. Place the packaged eggs in the hot water and cook for about 3 minutes, until the whites are set.
- Spoon the soup into four bowls, then unwrap the poached eggs and place one in the middle of each bowl.
- Finish with the anchovy fillets and a sprinkling of cayenne pepper.

DEEP-FRIED POTATO SKINS WITH ANCHOVY DIP

This is a great snack to make when you have potato skins left over from another dish. Make plenty as it is very more-ish.

¼ cup/2 fl oz/60 ml
mayonnaise
6 anchovy fillets, mashed
8 rosemary leaves, finely
chopped

olive oil
12 oz/375 g potato skins
sea salt and freshly ground
white pepper
a sprig of rosemary

- Mix the mayonnaise with the anchovies and rosemary, then season with a little white pepper.
- Heat about 2 in/5 cm olive oil in a heavy-bottomed pan to 325°F/170°C.
- Fry the potato skins until crisp and golden brown.
- Remove the skins from the oil and let drain on paper towels.
- Season the skins with sea salt, serve with the dip and garnish with the rosemary sprig.

ANCHOVIES WITH GNOCCHI AND SAGE

MAIN COURSE
SERVES 4

1 tin of anchovy fillets in olive oil (1¾ oz/50 g), drained
milk (to desalt the anchovies)
9 oz/250 g butter

1 bunch of sage, leaves separated
1 lb/16 oz/500 g gnocchi
1 tbsp chopped flat-leaf parsley
freshly ground white pepper

- Soak the anchovy fillets for a few minutes in lukewarm water or milk. Drain and pat dry.
- To clarify the butter, put the butter in a saucepan over medium heat and leave to melt completely, without allowing it to brown. Remove the pan from the heat. With a spoon, remove the milk solids from the butter.
- Place the pan back over medium heat and fry the sage leaves in the butter until crispy.
- Remove the pan from the heat, take out the leaves and let drain on paper towels.
- Cook the gnocchi in boiling water according to the package directions.
- Portion the gnocchi out onto four plates. Pour over the sage butter and sprinkle with parsley and white pepper.
- Add the crispy sage leaves and anchovies to the gnocchi and serve immediately.

BEEF TENDERLOIN WITH CHIMICHURRI

MAIN COURSE
SERVES 4

Chimichurri is a spicy Argentine sauce served with red meat. In this version, the anchovies and tomato paste add depth of flavor.

1 lb/16 oz/500 g beef tenderloin,
    cut into large pieces
2 red chiles, halved lengthwise
    and seeded
olive oil
2 tbsp tomato paste
1 tsp coarse sea salt
2 tsp black peppercorns
    (preferably first dry-toasted
    in a frying pan)

8 garlic cloves, crushed
2 tsp chopped oregano
2 sprigs of flat-leaf parsley
6 anchovy fillets
2 tsp red wine vinegar
skewers

- Take the meat out of the fridge half an hour before cooking. If you are using wooden or bamboo skewers, put them in cold water to soak.
- In a frying pan, bring about $1/4$ in/5 mm of water to a boil. Turn down the heat once it starts boiling, add the red chiles and boil for 5 minutes.
- Remove the chiles from the water and pat dry. Cut the flesh from the skin.
- Heat a splash of olive oil in the frying pan. Turn down the heat and add the tomato paste, stirring continuously for 1 minute. Remove from the heat.
- Put the salt, black peppercorns and garlic cloves in a mortar. Smash with a pestle until you have a thick paste. Add the red chiles, the herbs and the anchovies and smash into the paste. Add the tomato paste and the red wine vinegar.
- Thread the meat onto skewers and season with salt.
- Cook the meat on a hot grill for about 3 minutes, turning frequently, or until cooked to your liking.
- Serve the meat with the chimichurri sauce.

ANCHOVY AND OLIVE TART (PISSALADIÈRE)

MAIN COURSE
SERVES 4

1 tin of anchovy fillets in olive
  oil (1¾ oz/50 g), drained
olive oil
2 yellow onions, chopped
1 tsp sugar
1 sheet frozen puff pastry,
  thawed
½ cup/3½ oz/100 g black olives,
  pitted and halved

3½ oz/100 g Gruyère cheese,
  grated
1 egg yolk, lightly beaten
salt and freshly ground
  black pepper

- Preheat the oven to 350°F/180°C.
- Soak the anchovies in cold water for a few minutes to remove excess salt. Drain and lightly pat dry.
- Heat a splash of olive oil in a frying pan. Add the onions and sugar and fry over medium heat until lightly browned.
- Remove the onions from the heat and season with salt and pepper.
- Take the puff pastry and cut out a rectangle 10 in/25 cm wide by 16 in/40 cm long. Fold ½ in/1 cm of the edge over twice to make a border.
- Spread the onions over the puff pastry, leaving the border uncovered. Place the anchovies diagonally across the top. Sprinkle the olives and cheese over the top. Brush the edges of the puff pastry with the beaten egg yolk.
- Bake the anchovy tart in the oven for 15–20 minutes, until crisp and golden brown. Serve hot or warm.

SPECIES	Mussels
BINOMIAL NAME	*Mytilus edulis*
FISHING METHOD	Small-scale dredging
MSC CERTIFIED	Among others, Scottish mussels, Limfjord (Denmark), Oosterschelde (the Netherlands), Northern Ireland (for more information on the MSC, see page 6)
TINNED OPTIONS	Mussels in water, mussels in mustard-dill, mussels in chile-mango, smoked mussels

TO RETAIN FLAVOR, ADD MUSSELS TO A DISH ONLY AT THE LAST MINUTE.

MUSSELS

WHEREVER THERE ARE MUSSELS, there will be plenty of mussel farmers. They gather the mussel seed from the mussel beds and transfer them to their own plots, where they are cultivated to the desired size. Sustainable mussel-seed fishermen can be found in Zeeland in the Netherlands, the southwest of England and the Limfjord in Denmark. Their sustainable method is necessary, as mussel seed is becoming scarcer in many territories, like the Dutch Wadden Sea. The still-prevalent dredging method—in which heavy chain nets scrape the seabed—damages the natural habitats of other sea creatures. Alternative methods like the Zeeland fishermen's mussel seed–gathering systems are not just incredibly resourceful, their payoff is also very promising. The mussel seed is caught using net and rope structures and transported to the mussel plots at the bottom of the Eastern Scheldt in Zeeland, where over a few years they mature into delicious morsels.

This mussel seed–gathering technique is similar to that of the Spanish mussel fishers. Off the Galician coast, the fishermen build wooden structures with ropes. The mussel seed attaches itself to the ropes and is harvested when the mussels have grown large enough. It is also worth mentioning the pilings method, or *bouchot* technique, that is used off the coasts of Normandy and Brittany in France. There, during low tide, the mussel farmers attach cylindrical nets filled with mussel seed to poles on sandbanks out on the coast. Once the mussel seed has fully grown, the mussels are then harvested and presented to the consumer as *moules de bouchot*.

The larger mussels will find their way to the consumer fresh in the shell but a large part of the harvest will be preserved in tins and jars. Tinned mussels can come from anywhere, and they will generally hold the smaller mussels. Producers who add the MSC certification to their tins often include the fishing method and location on the packaging. Most other suppliers only include the prescribed number code, which at least ensures traceability.

Mussels in sauce are ready to eat as they are, savored with a simple chunk of bread. To retain the flavor when cooking mussels, add them to a dish only at the last minute.

MODERN TRADITIONAL FISHING TECHNIQUES DO THE JOB

Many Danish fishermen sail from Nykøbing harbor to the Limfjord in their colorful boats. They mostly sail alone, so the catch will be worth it financially. Poul Kaergaard takes a different approach; his two boats are manned by Erik and Mogens. They usually set out at 2 a.m. and come back around 4 p.m. the same day. They follow strict, self-imposed rules and only fish in areas of the fjord where the mussel population is strong. They often collaborate with biologists doing research in the area. This method works: after generations of mussel fishing, the mussel beds are still in a healthy condition, and their sustainable approach was awarded the MSC-certified label. To receive the MSC certification, the fishermen didn't need to change their way of fishing as their traditional fishing techniques already met the requirements perfectly.

SPANISH TOMATO RICE WITH MUSSELS

MAIN COURSE
SERVES 4

olive oil
2 bell peppers, seeded and cut
    into strips
5½ oz/150 g soft Spanish
    chorizo, sliced
2 large red onions, chopped
1 tbsp tomato paste
heaping 1½ cups/10½ oz/300 g
    Spanish paella rice
1 glass of dry white wine
8 garlic cloves, cut into large
    chunks

4 ripe tomatoes, peeled, seeded
    and chopped
6½ cups/52 fl oz/1.5 l chicken
    stock
1 tin of mussels in a spicy tomato
    sauce (4¼ oz/120 g)
freshly ground black pepper
juice of 1 lemon
1 bunch of cilantro, chopped

- Heat a dash of olive oil in a frying pan and fry the peppers over high heat for about 1 minute, stirring all the time. Remove from the pan and set aside.
- Reheat the pan and fry the chorizo over medium heat for a few minutes on each side. Remove from the pan and set aside.
- Pour the released fat out of the pan, but don't clean the pan.
- Gently fry the onions in the remaining chorizo oil.
- Add the tomato paste to the onion and cook for 1 minute.
- Add the rice and fry for 1 minute, stirring occasionally.
- Pour the wine into the pan and bring to a boil, stirring for 1 minute.
- Add the garlic, tomatoes and reserved peppers with enough of the chicken stock to just cover the rice. Bring to a simmer and simmer gently over low heat, stirring, until the stock has been absorbed.
- Add the remaining stock a little at a time, stirring, until the rice is just tender and the stock has been absorbed. The cooking time should be about 18 minutes (also see the package for cooking directions).
- When the rice is almost cooked, stir in the reserved chorizo and warm through, then add the mussels and black pepper and lemon juice to taste.
- Serve in four shallow bowls, garnished with the cilantro.

MUSSEL ESCABÈCHE WITH ROASTED PEPPERS

STARTER
SERVES 4

This is probably the simplest, cheapest and tastiest recipe in this book. When you find a Spanish food shop or a good fishmonger, do stock up on a couple of tins of *mejillones en escabèche*. They keep for years, so if you like the dish, it's worth buying a few. Escabèche is a spicy Spanish marinade made with paprika, pepper and vinegar or lemon. The sour taste goes well with the sweet mussels.

4 red bell peppers
3 tins of mussels in escabèche
 sauce (4¼ oz/120 g each)
2 tbsp mayonnaise

1 garlic clove, crushed
4 slices of white bread, toasted

- Preheat the broiler.
- Cut the peppers in half lengthwise. Place them cut-side down on parchment paper on a rack in a baking pan so that any excess liquid can flow freely. Put under the broiler and cook, turning once, until both sides are blistered and blackened but the flesh is still soft and juicy.
- Remove from the broiler and put in a sealed plastic container or bag to cool. When cool, remove the skin and seeds.
- Using a fork, mash the pepper flesh with the oil from 1 tin of mussels, the mayonnaise and the garlic.
- Stir in the mussels.
- Serve spread on the toast.

SPECIES Chum salmon, pink salmon and sockeye salmon

BINOMIAL NAMES *Oncorhynchus keta, Oncorhynchus gorbuscha* and *Oncorhynchus nerka*

FISHING METHODS Drift nets and purse seine

MSC CERTIFIED All salmon fisheries in Alaska and Canada, various in Russia (for more information on the MSC, see page 6)

TINNED OPTIONS Skinless and boneless salmon in water, salmon in water

ALASKAN FISHERIES HAVE BEEN WORKING UNDER STRICT CATCH REGULATIONS SINCE 1959.

SALMON

WHEN IT COMES TO TINNED SALMON, more and more varieties are becoming available: wild pink salmon, wild red salmon and farmed salmon, for example. The producer can also include the species on the label, which can be useful if you prefer the flavor of one over another. It's also good to know whether or not the salmon has been preserved with the bones. Heat softens the nutritious bones and makes them digestible. The skin is often also preserved in the tin with the salmon.

Wild salmon have to swim a lot during their lifetime and that shows through in the flesh, as the fat is more evenly distributed compared with farmed salmon. The wild salmon's firm flesh also generally has a stronger flavor. Farmed salmon can be found all over the world and European farming pools hold Atlantic salmon (*Salmo salar*), but it is highly unlikely you'll find Atlantic salmon in your tin as most tinned salmon is wild salmon from the coastal waters and rivers of Alaska. These seas and rivers are some of the cleanest in the world, which is important as the salmon's fat easily retains impurities.

Because the fisheries have been working under strict catch regulations since 1959, the existence of the Alaskan salmon is not threatened. For years, scientists and fishermen—often Inuit—have been keeping track of how many salmon swim to the spawning grounds each year. Based on these numbers, they determine the catch. This approach has earned them the coveted MSC certification.

Five types of salmon that are known by the general public under their native name are caught during the season: the light pink chum or keta salmon (*Oncorhynchus keta*) is generally the cheapest. The humpback salmon (*Oncorhynchus gorbuscha*) is sold as pink salmon. The coho or silver salmon (*Oncorhynchus kisutch*) is important to fishermen because of the high price they fetch. The best salmon swim up river in the spring. The fatty sockeye (*Oncorhynchus nerka*) or red salmon is available freshly smoked as well as tinned. The chinook or king salmon (*Oncorhynchus tshawytscha*) is the largest of the salmon family, and those caught are mainly destined for the smokehouses.

CHUM FROM THE YUKON AND PINK FROM THE POLAR STAR

In Alaska, both the indigenous people and other Americans fish for salmon with an MSC certification and are bound by strict catch regulations. In summer, Yup'ik Eskimo Maxine casts her nets from her small boat into the fast-flowing Yukon, in the hope of catching lots of chum salmon which, according to Maxine, is the best salmon available.

One of the 6,200 inhabitants of Kodiak Island, Pat Pikus takes a different approach to salmon fishing: he sails out to open sea and uses ring nets. Fellow fishermen see Pat as one of the best salmon fishermen in Alaska. He catches pink salmon, sailing his family's boat the *Polar Star*. The fishermen named the pink salmon after a village at the foot of the narrow Aleutian mountain range, an isthmus reaching a different time zone in the Pacific Ocean. Fishermen like Pat, who use ring nets in this part of Alaska, strictly adhere to the catch restrictions. A portion of his catch is destined for the Ocean Beauty cannery in Seattle, the same cannery where the Fish Tales tins are manufactured. Salmon fishing on the open sea in these tempestuous parts of the Pacific is not without its dangers. Pat and his men regularly save people from drowning in the freezing cold water.

SALMON TARTARE WITH SOFT-BOILED EGGS AND GREEN ONIONS

STARTER
SERVES 4

2 tins of pink or red salmon,
boneless and skinless
(6 oz/170 g each), drained
5 tbsp (3 fl oz/80 ml)
mayonnaise

2 eggs, soft-boiled, chopped
3 green onions, roughly chopped
freshly ground black pepper
4 slices of sourdough bread,
toasted

- Mash the salmon with the mayonnaise to make a creamy tartare, then spoon onto a plate.
- Arrange the eggs on the tartare and sprinkle with the green onions. Season with black pepper.
- Serve with toasted sourdough bread.

SALMON, LEEK AND CREAM CHEESE QUICHE

STARTER/MAIN COURSE
SERVES 4

2 leeks, white parts only, cut in half
  lengthwise and thinly sliced
1 tbsp olive oil
a dash of white wine
3 eggs, beaten
generous 1 cup/9 fl oz/250 ml
  whipping cream

2 tins of pink or red salmon
  (6 oz/170 g each), drained
1 oz/30 g butter, melted
8 sheets frozen puff pastry, thawed
5½ oz/150 g cream cheese
3½ oz/100 g mixed greens
salt and freshly ground black pepper

- Preheat the oven to 350°F/180°C and grease a 10 in/25 cm cake pan.
- Fry the leeks in the oil over low heat until soft but not browned.
- Add the wine and bring to a boil, stirring to mix in the juices.
- Mix the eggs, cream, and salmon and season with salt and pepper, then stir in the leeks.
- Line the pan with the puff pastry, prick the bottom with a fork and bake for 8 minutes. Remove from the oven and press to flatten the bottom.
- Pour the egg-cream mixture into the base and dot with the cream cheese.
- Bake for 30 minutes, until set and golden brown. Serve with the greens.

POTATO AND LEEK SOUP WITH RED SALMON

STARTER
SERVES 4

5 leeks, white parts only
1¾ oz/50 g butter
3 floury potatoes, such as russet
  or Kennebec, peeled and
  cut into chunks
1⅔ cups/14 fl oz/400 ml
  chicken stock
ice cubes
1 tin of pink or red salmon,
  boneless and skinless
  (6 oz/170 g), drained and
  cut into chunks

1 red bell pepper, seeded and
  thinly sliced
1 handful of chives, finely
  chopped
salt and freshly ground white
  pepper

- Chop 4 of the leeks. The remaining leek will serve as a garnish.
- Heat the butter in a deep, heavy-bottomed pan, add the leeks and braise until soft, without allowing them to brown.
- Add the potatoes and chicken stock to the pan, bring to a simmer and cook on low heat until the potatoes are tender.
- Meanwhile, bring a pan of water to a boil while you cut the remaining leek into thin rings. Parboil the leek in boiling water for 1 minute, then drain and put into a bowl of iced water.
- Season the soup with salt and white pepper. Heat the soup thoroughly and purée until frothy with an immersion blender.
- Spoon the soup into bowls and add the salmon, then garnish with the sliced pepper, leek rings and chives.

SALMON SPREAD WITH SOURDOUGH BREAD

STARTER/MAIN COURSE
SERVES 2–4

2 tins of pink or red salmon,
   boneless and skinless
   (6 oz/170 g each), drained
   and cut into chunks
3 tbsp mayonnaise
2 tbsp whipping cream, beaten
   to soft peaks

1 tsp cayenne pepper
1 tsp finely grated lemon zest
1 green onion, thinly sliced
1 tbsp lemon juice
salt and freshly ground black
   pepper
4 slices of sourdough bread,
   toasted if you like

- Mash the salmon in a bowl. Add the mayonnaise, whipped cream and cayenne pepper and mix to a fairly smooth consistency.
- Add the lemon zest and the green onion. Season with lemon juice, salt and pepper.
- Spread on the sourdough slices and serve.

SPECIES	Mackerel
BINOMIAL NAME	*Scomber scombrus*
FISHING METHODS	Drift nets and purse seine
MSC CERTIFIED	Certification has been temporarily suspended because the countries involved could not reach an agreement on quota. The stocks are healthy. Talks were held in 2014, but there is currently no clarity on whether the MSC suspension will be lifted in the near future (for more information on the MSC, see page 6)
TINNED OPTIONS	Steamed mackerel in water, mackerel in oil, smoked mackerel in oil, mackerel in sauce, mackarel with black pepper

IN SALADS, MACKEREL IS A GOOD SUBSTITUTE FOR THE OFTEN-USED TUNA AND SALMON.

MACKEREL

IN THE SUPERMARKET AISLES, you'll find many varieties of tinned mackerel: steamed mackerel in water, mackerel in oil, smoked mackerel in oil, mackerel in sauce, mackerel with black pepper; the fish is apparently popular. And rightly so, because the delicious, oily mackerel is a source of healthy omega-3 fatty acids and other nutrients. It is also a very versatile fish in both its natural and smoked forms and goes well with many flavors. For example, in salads, mackerel is a good substitute for the often-used tuna and salmon.

Neutral-flavored pieces of mackerel fillet are initially briefly sterilized with a small amount of salt. To make mackerel in sauce, the fish processors first place the mackerel in a brine and then steam the fish in a tin without a lid. It is then drained of excess water, the tin is filled with a sauce and covered with a lid. The tins are then sterilized. Even smoked mackerel is first brined before being smoked in a smoking chamber, after which the oil is added. The tin is then covered and ready for sterilization.

Japan produces extraordinary mackerel, prepared with ginger and typically Japanese ingredients like miso. Connoisseurs believe this mackerel is best served on its own rather than mixed with other flavors. This book doesn't feature any recipes with Japanese mackerel, although if you want to try it, it is available on the Internet.

The fat content of the mackerel depends on the fishing season, which itself varies depending on the latitude and the type of mackerel. The fish processor will take this into account because you get better

results if you smoke a fatty mackerel rather than a lean one. Mackerel from the Northern Hemisphere is lean around May, when the fish have just spawned. In summer and early autumn, the mackerel fill themselves up with food, so from October onward the fishermen can start to haul in these big boys.

More and more fisheries are turning to stock-saving techniques and show a willingness to return unwanted bycatch to the sea. North Atlantic mackerel fishing had been MSC-certified for years, but since 2013 the certificate has been temporarily suspended, and mackerel fishermen have no longer been allowed to carry the certification label. The reason for this is that countries with uncertified fisheries, like Iceland, were also fishing the same areas, which meant that more mackerel was being caught than had been agreed in the quotas. Negotiations are necessary to ensure that fisheries will all adhere to the requirements. Having said that, the mackerel populations in these areas is nonetheless healthy.

MACKEREL WITH STIR-FRIED VEGETABLES AND CHILE SAUCE

MAIN COURSE
SERVES 4

7 oz/200 g sugar snap peas or
    snow peas
7 oz/200 g broccolini, cut
    lengthwise
about 2 tbsp sesame oil
2 yellow onions, chopped
1 tsp soy sauce

2 tins of mackerel fillets in olive
    oil (4½ oz/125 g each),
    drained
1¾ oz/50 g sprouts
chile sauce
salt and freshly ground black
    pepper

- Bring a pan of lightly salted water to a boil, add the sugar snap peas and boil for a few minutes, until just tender, then drain, reserving the water.
- Return the water to a boil and blanch the broccolini in the same way. Drain and pat dry.
- Put a wok over high heat, add a dash of sesame oil and fry the onions until golden brown. Remove them from the wok.
- Add a little more sesame oil to the pan and fry the sugar snaps and broccolini over high heat until hot and coated in oil.
- Add the fried onions and stir, then add the soy sauce and stir everything together until hot.
- Remove the wok from the heat and season the vegetables with black pepper.
- Divide the vegetables among four plates and place the mackerel on top of the vegetables.
- Add the sprouts and serve with chile sauce.

PEKING MACKEREL

SNACK/STARTER
SERVES 4

2 Little Gem lettuces
½ cup/4 oz/250 g hoisin sauce
1 ripe mango, cut into
    small slices
1 cucumber, peeled, seeded and
    cut into thin strips
1 bunch of green onions,
    white parts only, cut
    into thin strips

1 tin of smoked mackerel fillets,
    (4½ oz/125 g each),
    drained and flaked
1 small piece of fresh ginger,
    peeled and grated

- Remove the outer leaves of the Little Gems, then remove the hearts, to create little cups.
- In each lettuce cup, spoon 1 teaspoon of hoisin sauce.
- Place a slice of mango in each cup. Add the strips of cucumber and green onion.
- Add the pieces of mackerel to the cups.
- To finish, sprinkle a little of the grated ginger on top of the mackerel.

SMOKED MACKEREL, MASH AND RELISH

STARTER
SERVES 4

14 oz/400 g potatoes
3½ oz/100 g cold butter, cut
*   into cubes*
scant ½ cup/3½ fl oz/100 ml
*   hot milk*
sea salt

a pinch of freshly grated nutmeg
1 tin of smoked mackerel fillets
*   (4½ oz/125 g each),*
*   drained*
1 jar of relish, such as lime
*   pickle or piccalilli*

- Bring a large pan of water to a boil and boil the potatoes in their skins until just tender.
- Drain, leave until cool enough to handle, then peel the potatoes, reserving the skins for Deep-Fried Potato Skins with Anchovy Dip on page 52.
- Mash the potato flesh with a potato ricer or masher, beat in the cold butter with a spatula, then stir in the hot milk. Season with salt and nutmeg.
- Ladle the mashed potatoes onto four plates.
- Place the pieces of mackerel on top and serve with relish.

SMOKED MACKEREL WITH BRAISED LEEKS

STARTER
SERVES 4

scant ¼ cup/10 z/30 g pine nuts
4 medium leeks, white part only
olive oil
scant ½ cup/3½ fl oz/100 ml
    chicken stock
3 tbsp white wine vinegar
3 tbsp sunflower oil

1 tbsp Dijon mustard
2 tins of smoked mackerel fillets
    (4½ oz/125 g each)
a few sprigs of tarragon, leaves
    separated
salt and freshly ground
    black pepper

- Heat a frying pan over medium heat and dry toast the pine nuts for a few minutes until lightly browned. Set aside.
- Remove the outer leaves of the leeks. Cut the leeks in half and then cut in half lengthwise.
- Heat a generous splash of olive oil in a frying pan. Turn the heat down to low and place the leeks cut side down in the oil.
- Add a splash of chicken stock and leave the leeks to cook gently for about 15 minutes, until they are tender when pierced with a sharp knife, turning once during cooking.
- Put the vinegar, sunflower oil, mustard, salt and pepper in a bowl and beat with a fork or whisk into a vinaigrette.
- Divide the leeks among four plates. Place the mackerel on top of the leeks and spoon the vinaigrette over the dish.
- Garnish with pine nuts and tarragon leaves.

MACKEREL WITH WATERCRESS

MAIN COURSE
SERVES 4

7 oz/200 g waxy potatoes
olive oil
2 tbsp white wine vinegar
1 tbsp Dijon mustard
3½ oz/100 g watercress
2 tins of mackerel fillets in olive
oil (4½ oz/125 g each),
drained

1¾ oz/50 g sprouts
sea salt and freshly ground
white pepper

- Bring a large pan of water to a boil and boil the potatoes in their skins until just tender.
- Drain, then roughly crush the potatoes with a drizzle of olive oil and season with salt and white pepper.
- Put the vinegar, a splash of olive oil, the mustard and a pinch of salt in a bowl and whisk into a vinaigrette.
- Toss the watercress with the vinaigrette and place on four plates. Add the crushed potatoes, then the mackerel and garnish with the sprouts.

MACKEREL, BEETS, APPLE AND PICKLE REMOULADE

STARTER
SERVES 4

2 tbsp Dijon mustard
1 tbsp red wine vinegar, plus
    extra for seasoning
a dash of Worcestershire sauce
¼ cup/2 fl oz/60 ml olive oil
1 shallot, finely chopped
2 cooked beets
1 crisp green apple, such as
    Granny Smith
2 pickled gherkins

generous 1 cup/9 fl oz/250 ml
    sour cream
2 tbsp finely chopped chives
2 tins of smoked mackerel
    fillets (4½ oz/125 g each),
    drained and flaked
salt and freshly ground
    black pepper

- Use a fork to beat the mustard, vinegar, Worcestershire sauce, olive oil and shallot into a vinaigrette, seasoning with salt and pepper.
- Cut the beets, apple and gherkins into ¼ in/5 mm cubes.
- Add the vinaigrette to the cubes and season with salt and pepper, if necessary.
- Mix the sour cream with some salt, pepper, a few drops of red wine vinegar and the chives. Stir in the smoked mackerel.
- Put equal amounts of the smoked mackerel and beets on four plates and serve.

SPECIES	Sardine
BINOMIAL NAME	*Sardina pilchardus*
FISHING METHOD	Purse seine
MSC CERTIFIED	South Brittany (France) and Cornwall (UK) (for more information on the MSC see page 6). Portugese sardine fishery temporarily suspended while stocks recover.
TINNED OPTIONS	Sardines in water, sardines in olive oil, sardines in tomato sauce, sardine fillets in olive oil

THE PORTUGUESE CONSIDER THEIR TINNED SARDINES TO BE THE ABSOLUTE FINEST.

SARDINES

SARDINES COME IN ALL SIZES. On land they are arranged by size in factories by skillful hands or machines so that similarly sized sardines are tinned together. The larger sardines that don't fit into the small tins after decapitation will be cut into pieces and processed as fillets. The really tiny ones are used in spreads or as fish feed.

Fans of these little squirts won't be forgotten. Some producers offer them as *sardinella*, a delicious tapas dish. In a bar somewhere in Spain, after a glass of white wine, you can get into a heated discussion about sardines. Is the *sardinella* actually a sardine? The bartender will set you straight: of course it's a real sardine. After all it's a member of the same family—the mouth of the sardine doesn't extend as far as its cousin's, the anchovy. He'll be able to tell you about *sardinops* (South American pilchards) and that the English regard the pilchard as the true sardine. And sardines are also related to herring, he'll add. You could find yourself entering a seemingly endless discussion, so it's probably advisable to leave scientific classification as a topic and steer the conversation into a culinary direction—which is hard enough, because how should you serve sardines as a tapas dish? One person swears by lemon, the other prefers the fish with the finest olive oil. And why not add a *salsa picante*?

Sardines have been tinned for nearly 200 years. In the nineteenth century the tinned fish was regarded as a delicacy by the upper classes. Because the soft fish disintegrated almost immediately when picked out of the tin with a fork, a cutlery manufacturer developed the sardine fork with blunt prongs, and collectors will readily pay high prices for antique examples. A well-preserved sardine fork even got a display spot in the Central Museum of Utrecht.

A few European countries have a true tradition of tinning sardines. You should buy sardines from a reputable brand, keep in a cool place outside the fridge and turn regularly to ensure the fish doesn't dry out on one side.

According to the French, sardines were first tinned along the south coast of Brittany, and there are still many factories along the coast making tinned sardines, often in sauce. One of the oldest recipes is *sardines au beurre*, often a *beurre de baratte*, a farmhouse butter. A typically French custom is to heat the tin in hot water, then open it and eat the sardines with more melted butter, baby potatoes and lettuce. Another French tradition is to mature the sardines in the tin, which enhances the flavor of the fish.

The treatment of the sardines also determines the quality of the tinned product. In this respect, North Portuguese producer A Poveira sets the standards by its good practice. The Portuguese consider their tinned sardines to be the absolute best. A Poveira uses only the freshest sardines that come in daily and are cut and tinned by hand in the workshop (also see page 17).

Sardine levels are healthy in certain waters. To ensure the continuing safety of the stock populations, a number of fisheries—from Cornwall and South Brittany to name a few—had themselves certified by the MSC. These fisheries operate under catch restrictions and strict fishing methods.

SARDINES AND BURRATA WITH ROASTED VEGETABLES

STARTER
SERVES 4

Use the best-quality burrata, if you can, made with buffalo mozzarella and cream. If you can't get burrata, use buffalo mozzarella or ordinary mozzarella.

1 zucchini, sliced
1 red bell pepper, seeded
    and sliced
1 yellow bell pepper, seeded
    and sliced
1 eggplant, sliced
2 red onions, quartered
olive oil
1 soft Spanish chorizo (or a
    4 in/10 cm piece of hard
    Spanish chorizo), cut
    into chunks

9 oz/250 g cherry tomatoes
3 garlic cloves, roughly chopped
1 burrata or mozzarella, diced
    or crumbled
2 tins of sardines in water or
    olive oil (4¼ oz/120 g
    each), drained
coarse sea salt and freshly
    ground black pepper
1 lemon, cut into wedges

- Preheat the oven to 350°F/180°C.
- Drizzle the zucchini, peppers, eggplant, and onions with olive oil and roast for 20 minutes.
- Meanwhile, heat a splash of olive oil in a frying pan and fry the chorizo for a moment. Remove from the pan and drain half of the released fat. Set the chorizo aside.
- Fry the tomatoes and chopped garlic in the fatty juices over medium heat until just softened.
- Turn off the heat and return the chorizo to the pan.
- Place the vegetables, tomatoes and chorizo on a large plate.
- Place the burrata or mozzarella on the vegetables.
- Season with sea salt and black pepper.
- Serve with the sardines and lemon wedges.

SARDINE AND TWO-CHEESE CROSTINI

SNACK/STARTER
SERVES 4

1 tin of sardines in water or olive
    oil (4¼ oz/120 g), drained
7 oz/200 g cherry tomatoes
olive oil
1 tsp tomato paste
1 yellow onion, chopped
1 tsp balsamic vinegar
a couple of cabbage leaves
3½ oz/100 g spinach, rinsed
    and dried

grilled or toasted baguette slices
3½ oz/100 g Parmesan cheese,
    shaved
3½ oz/100 g tangy soft goat's
    cheese, crumbled
salt and freshly ground
    black pepper
a few chives, finely chopped

- Mash the sardines with a fork, then cover and set aside in the fridge.
- Cut the cherry tomatoes in half and remove the seeds.
- Heat a splash of olive oil in a frying pan and stir in the tomato paste.
- Place the tomatoes, cut side down, in the oil. Add the onion and balsamic vinegar. Turn down the heat and cook the tomatoes until the skins are shriveled and the cut side has colored slightly. Remove the pan from the heat and leave the tomatoes to cool.
- Gently remove the skins from the tomatoes.
- Roughly crush the tomatoes with the onion and oil. Season with salt and pepper.
- Cut and remove the center vein of the cabbage leaves and cut the leaves into strips. Heat a splash of olive oil in a large frying pan and quickly cook the cabbage over high heat until just wilted.
- Heat a splash of olive oil in a second large frying pan and quickly cook the spinach over high heat. Drain off any excess liquid, if necessary.
- Place the tomato salsa on some of the crostini. Lay the sardines and cabbage leaf on the tomatoes and sprinkle with Parmesan cheese.
- Place the remaining sardines on the other crostini, add some spinach and goat's cheese and garnish with chives.

TARTARE OF SARDINE WITH TOMATO CARPACCIO

STARTER
SERVES 4

2 tins of sardines in olive oil
   (4¼ oz/120 g each),
   drained
2 tbsp capers, rinsed and finely
   chopped
3 tbsp sun-dried tomatoes, finely
   chopped
3 tbsp pitted black olives, finely
   chopped

1 bunch of basil, leaves torn
2 red tomatoes, sliced
2 orange tomatoes, sliced
2 yellow tomatoes, sliced
2 green tomatoes, sliced
1¾ oz/50 g soft goat's cheese
good-quality olive oil
sea salt and freshly ground
   white pepper

- Using a fork, mash the sardines, then mix with the capers, sun-dried tomatoes, olives and some of the basil to create the tartare.
- Place the tartare in the middle of a large plate.
- Arrange the tomato slices around the tartare.
- Crumble the goat's cheese over the tomatoes and sprinkle with some basil.
- Drizzle some olive oil over the tomatoes.
- Season with sea salt and white pepper to finish.

SARDINES WITH THYME-TOMATO CONFIT

STARTER
SERVES 4

Pungent garlic adds just enough flavor to this simple, fresh sauce without overpowering the dish and allows the sardines to shine as the main ingredient. Use less garlic for a more mild sauce.

7 oz/200 g cherry tomatoes
olive oil
8 garlic cloves, roughly chopped
a few sprigs of thyme, finely chopped
½ tsp balsamic vinegar

2 tins of sardines or sardinella in olive oil (4¼ oz/120 g each), drained
sea salt and freshly ground black pepper

- Cut the cherry tomatoes in half and remove the seeds.
- Heat a dash of olive oil in a large frying pan and place the tomatoes, cut side down, into the pan. Add the garlic and a little thyme. Turn down the heat and leave the tomatoes to slowly absorb the flavors.
- Once the skins are shriveled and the cut side has colored slightly, remove the pan from the heat and leave the tomatoes to cool.
- Gently remove the skins from the tomatoes. This should be easy if the tomatoes are completely cooked.
- Crush the tomatoes with the garlic and olive oil. Season with the vinegar, salt and pepper.
- Spoon the tomatoes on to plates, top with sardines or *sardinella* and sprinkle with a little more thyme, if you like.

SARDINES WITH PAPAS AND MOJO SAUCE

STARTER
SERVES 4

2 Romano or red bell peppers
3 small dried red chiles
2 tsp cumin seeds
1 tsp coriander seeds
8 garlic cloves, chopped
olive oil
2 tbsp red wine vinegar
1 tsp paprika

scant ½ cup/3½ oz/100 g
    sea salt, plus extra for
    seasoning
9 oz/250 g baby potatoes in
    their skins
2 tins of sardines in olive oil
    (4¼ oz/120 g each),
    drained

- Preheat the broiler.
- Cut the peppers in half lengthwise and remove the seeds, place them on a rack with the skin side up and broil until the skin has blistered and blackened and the flesh is soft. Cover and leave to cool.
- Remove the skin and cut the flesh into thin strips. Set aside.
- Fill a small frying pan with water and bring to a boil. Remove the stems from the red chiles. Cut them lengthwise and remove the seeds. Place the chiles in the water and cook for a few minutes, until soft.
- Remove the chiles from the water and pat dry. Scrape the flesh from the skin with a knife.
- Heat a frying pan and dry toast the cumin and coriander seeds for a minute or so.
- Using a mortar and pestle, grind the cumin and coriander seeds, then mix them with the peppers, chiles, garlic cloves and a generous dash of olive oil. Season with the vinegar, some more olive oil, paprika and a pinch of salt. Set the mojo aside.
- Add the salt to a pan of boiling water and cook the baby potatoes until tender. Remove the potatoes from the water using a slotted spoon and leave to cool. They're ready to eat when coated with a white salt residue.
- Serve the sardines with the mojo and the potatoes.

SARDINE AND GARLIC MASH

SNACK/STARTER
SERVES 4

1 head garlic
¼ cup/2 fl oz/60 ml olive oil,
    plus extra for drizzling
5½ oz/150 g potatoes, peeled
4 eggs
2 tins of sardines in water or
    olive oil (4¼ oz/120 g
    each), drained

1 tbsp chopped flat-leaf parsley
1 tbsp lemon juice
sea salt and freshly ground
    black pepper
crusty bread

- Preheat the oven to 350°F/180°C.
- Drizzle the head of garlic with olive oil and wrap in aluminum foil. Roast the garlic for 30–40 minutes, until soft. Gently squeeze the cloves out of the papery skin. Use four or however many you like. Keep the rest to use in other dishes.
- Boil the potatoes in salted water until tender, then drain.
- Meanwhile, boil the eggs for 8 minutes, then drain, rinse in cold water and leave to cool.
- Roughly crush the potatoes with a fork.
- Peel the eggs and mash with a fork.
- Mash the sardines with a fork.
- Combine the potatoes, eggs and sardines with the olive oil and most of the parsley. Season with lemon juice, salt and pepper.
- Garnish with garlic cloves, sprinkle with the remaining parsley and serve with crusty bread.

SARDINE BITES WITH WHITE BEAN PURÉE AND BASIL OIL

SNACK/STARTER
SERVES 4

10 fresh basil leaves, plus extra
    for serving
3 tbsp olive oil
sea salt
a splash of lime juice
9 oz/250 g cooked butter beans
1 tbsp mayonnaise
3 tbsp olive oil

10 sun-dried tomatoes,
    finely chopped
2 tins of sardines in water or
    olive oil (4¼ oz/120 g
    each), drained
thin crispbreads
sea salt and freshly ground
    black pepper

- First make the basil oil. Using a food processor or immersion blender, mix the basil leaves and oil. (If you use a mortar and pestle to combine the basil with some salt, pepper and oil, your result will be a creamier texture and flavor.)
- Season with some lime juice.
- Put the beans in a colander and rinse. Leave to drain. Purée the beans with the mayonnaise and olive oil.
- Stir in the sun-dried tomatoes. Season with salt and pepper.
- Place the sardines on the crispbreads.
- Top with the white bean purée, drizzle some basil oil over the top and sprinkle with sea salt. Garnish with some torn basil leaves.

SARDINE BITES WITH CHICKPEA PURÉE AND ROASTED GARLIC

SNACK/STARTER
SERVES 4

25 garlic cloves, peeled
olive oil
1 red onion, chopped
9 oz/250 g cooked chickpeas,
*   rinsed and drained*
sesame oil
grated zest and juice of 1 lime

2 tins of sardines in water or
*   olive oil (4¼ oz/120 g*
*   each), drained*
sea salt and freshly ground
*   black pepper*
thin crispbreads
cayenne pepper

- Preheat the oven to 350°F/180°C.
- Put the garlic cloves in a piece of aluminum foil, drizzle with some olive oil and season with salt and pepper. Fold over the top and roast for 20 minutes, until completely soft. Squeeze one of the cloves to check that they are done. Remove the foil packet from the oven.
- Heat a splash of olive oil in a frying pan and fry the onion over medium heat until just colored. Remove from the pan and set aside.
- Put the chickpeas in a bowl and add 5 roasted garlic cloves. Mix into a loose purée with a dash of sesame oil, some lime juice, salt and pepper to taste.
- Roughly mash the sardines with a dash of olive oil.
- Place the onions on the crispbreads and top with the sardines.
- Spoon some chickpea purée onto the sardines and press the roasted garlic cloves into the purée.
- To finish, garnish the crispbreads with some sea salt, cayenne pepper and lime zest.

SPECIES	Snow crab and red king crab
BINOMIAL NAMES	*Paralithodes camtschaticus* and *Chionoecetes opilio*
FISHING METHODS	Traps and pots
MSC CERTIFIED	Nova Scotia, Gulf of St Lawrence and Newfoundland and Labrador (Canada) (for more information on the MSC, see page 6)
TINNED OPTION	Crabmeat in water

CRABMEAT FROM THE CLAWS IS FLAVORSOME AND WELL SUITED TO SOUPS AND SAUCES.

CRAB

THE RED KING CRAB IS THE ONLY CRAB whose name is proudly used on the labels of tins. This has to do with the limited supply available of this crab. The crab—with its claws like garden shears—hails from Alaskan waters and is the star of the popular Discovery Channel program *Deadliest Catch*. American fishermen bring in these sturdy crabs, frequently measuring more than a meter in size, from the freezing Bering Sea. The crab is very profitable, so the fishermen literally cram as many as they can into the hold.

The red king crab finds its way to the consumer both fresh and frozen, but also in tins and jars. The Russians also catch this crab, and most of their meat is destined for the Chatka cannery in Spain. Hunks of red king crabmeat would be an assault on your weekly shopping budget— tinned crab doesn't get better than this, although this level of quality comes at a price. Several producers specializing in fish are particularly known for supplying tins with crab of this quality.

Other countries, however, like Chile, export more competitively priced tinned red king crab. In some areas, you can also buy cheaper tinned crabmeat, commonly known as "extra fancy" or "special," which contains some claw meat. This crab comes from Southeast Asia. Fancy crabmeat is perfectly fine to drain and use in crab cakes, soups, salads and quesadillas.

Countries where a lot of crab is consumed offer meat of varying quality. Lump, one large piece or several slightly smaller pieces, is the highest quality, then "special," which might be of lower quality but is preferable in taste and structure to surimi, imitation crabmeat made from pressed whitefish meat. Producers also offer just meat from the claws, which is darker in color and very flavorful. This meat is well suited to soups and sauces.

Crab is also available to the consumer in both MSC-certified and uncertified tins. Crab from certified fisheries in Canada will partly be sold with the blue MSC label.

Good-quality snow crab is available from the fishermen of the Canadian Nova Scotia peninsula. The smaller snow crab is also quite expensive. The fishermen catch the crabs in cage traps. Part of the catch won't leave the island—tourists eat the crabs in restaurants along one the world's most beautiful coastal roads, the Cabot Trail. The tranquil Nova Scotia has so much to offer, you find yourself wondering why people go out to sea. It must be the fishermen's hunting instinct.

PLANTAIN, CRAB AND MANGO CHUTNEY

SNACK/STARTER
SERVES 4

For a tasty alternative, use smoked mackerel, smoked mussels or kippers instead of crab.

1 tin of crabmeat (6 oz/170 g), drained	sunflower oil
1 tbsp mayonnaise	1 jar of mango chutney, preferably Sharwood's
1 lime	cayenne pepper
1 plantain	a few chives, finely chopped
1 tbsp all-purpose flour, sifted	crispy fried onions

- Mix the crab with the mayonnaise and a few drops of lime juice.
- Cut the plantain into slices ¼ in (6 mm) thick.
- Put the flour on a sheet of plastic wrap. Flour both sides of the plantain slices and place them in one layer on the plastic wrap. Place another layer of plastic wrap on top. Use a pan to press down lightly on the plantain to make the slices a bit thinner.
- Heat a little oil in a large frying pan and fry the slices until crisp and golden brown. This should take about a minute. Use paper towels to pat dry and drain excess oil.
- Place a teaspoon of mango chutney on each slice.
- Spoon the crab on top of the mango chutney.
- Sprinkle with cayenne pepper, the chives and the crispy fried onions.

CRAB SALAD WITH ORANGE AND FENNEL

STARTER
SERVES 4

juice of 1 orange
juice of ½ lime
¼ cup/2 fl oz/60 ml
*   mayonnaise*
3 Little Gems or 1 romaine
*   lettuce*
2 oranges, peeled and cut into
*   segments*

1 baby fennel bulb, cut into
*   thin strips*
2 tins of crabmeat (6 oz/170 g
*   each), drained*
a handful of basil
sea salt and freshly ground
*   white pepper*

- Beat together the orange and lime juices, the mayonnaise, salt and white pepper to make a dressing.
- Remove and discard the outer leaves of the lettuce and detach the lettuce leaves from the hearts. Arrange on a plate.
- Put the orange segments, the fennel strips and the crab on the lettuce leaves.
- Drizzle the dressing over the salad and garnish with small basil leaves.

CRAB WITH APPLE AND CURRY-GINGER SAUCE

STARTER
SERVES 4

1 celery rib
3 tart apples, such as Granny
    Smith
1 tin of crabmeat (6 oz/170 g),
    drained
1 tbsp curry powder

¼ cup/2 fl oz/60 ml
    mayonnaise
1¼ in/3 cm piece of fresh ginger,
    peeled and grated
cayenne pepper

- With a knife, pull off the tough fibrous strings of the celery, then cut the celery into thin crescent shapes.
- Peel 1 apple and cut into cubes.
- Take the crabmeat from the tin and set aside a little bit of the meat for garnish.
- Mix the remaining crabmeat with the curry powder, mayonnaise, apple cubes, grated ginger and part of the celery. Season with cayenne pepper.
- From the top and bottom of the remaining 2 apples, cut slices about ⅛ in/3 mm thick.
- Place the crab salad on the apple slices. Garnish with the reserved crabmeat, some cayenne pepper and the remaining celery.

MUSHROOMS WITH CRAB, GARLIC AND GRUYÈRE

MAIN COURSE
SERVES 4

20 large white mushrooms
juice of 1 lemon
2 tins of crabmeat (6 oz/170 g
    each), drained
2 tbsp olive oil
1 tbsp very finely chopped garlic
2 tbsp finely chopped flat-leaf
    parsley

cayenne pepper
3½ oz/100 g Gruyère cheese,
    grated
2 tbsp finely chopped chives
sea salt

- Preheat the oven to 375°F/190°C.
- Cut the stems off the mushrooms (use them later for a soup).
- Bring a large saucepan of water to a boil with the lemon juice and a pinch of salt.
- Add the mushroom caps and boil for 2 minutes.
- Remove from the pan and leave the mushrooms to drain on a kitchen towel.
- Combine the crab, olive oil, garlic, parsley, a pinch of cayenne pepper and, if necessary, a little salt.
- Put the mushrooms, gill sides up, in a baking dish, fill them with the crab mixture and sprinkle the grated Gruyère on top.
- Bake the mushrooms in the oven for about 7 minutes. If necessary, place under the broiler to add some color to the cheese.
- Sprinkle the chives over the mushrooms and serve.

CRAB WITH MANGO, AVOCADO AND GRATED GINGER

STARTER
SERVES 4

6 oranges
juice of 1 lime
1 tsp Thai fish sauce (nam pla)
2 tsp sesame oil
1 tsp soy sauce
1 ripe mango, peeled and
thinly sliced

2 ripe avocados, pitted and
thinly sliced
2 tins of crabmeat (6 oz/170 g
each), drained
1¼ in/3 cm piece of fresh ginger,
peeled and grated
cayenne pepper

- Cut some strips of orange zest using a vegetable peeler. Be careful not to peel the white pith as it has a bitter taste.
- Squeeze the oranges and pass the juice through a sieve.
- Put the juice and zest strips in a pan. Bring to a boil, then boil to reduce by half. Make sure the juice doesn't turn brown (color in the juice indicates caramelization of the sugars, which you do not want in this dish).
- Leave the orange juice to cool, then chill in the fridge.
- Take the juice out of the fridge, remove the zest and add a bit of lime juice.
- With a fork, beat in the fish sauce, sesame oil and soy sauce.
- Pour the dressing into four bowls.
- Place the mango, avocado and crab in each bowl.
- Place a tiny dollop of grated ginger on top and sprinkle with cayenne pepper to serve.

SPECIES	Cockles
BINOMIAL NAME	*Cerastoderma edule*
FISHING METHOD	Hand raking
MSC CERTIFIED	Dee Estuary and Bury Estuary (United Kingdom), the Wadden Sea (the Netherlands) (for more information on the MSC, see page 6)
TINNED OPTION	Cockles in water

A GLASS OF SALTY MANZANILLA SHERRY MAKES FOR A GOOD ACCOMPANIMENT TO COCKLES.

COCKLES

SPANIARDS LOVE SHELLFISH. You won't find a tapas night without mussels, clams and cockles. These shellfish are in high demand. If fresh shellfish aren't available, they'll happily make do with tinned versions. Tinned cockles are great because after harvest they're immediately cooked in their own juices and packaged. The cooking liquid is salty, and some sandy sediment is not uncommon. A glass of salty manzanilla makes for a good accompaniment to cockles. This sherry from the southern Spanish coast is aged in open storehouses where the sea salt–heavy Atlantic winds blow freely.

Many cockles—the *berberechos*—are harvested off the Galician coast in northern Spain, but the catch is not sufficient to supply the high demand. The Spanish have found an ally in the Dutch, who themselves prefer imported *vongole* to their own fleshy cockles from the Wadden Sea. Perhaps a *spaghetti alle cardidi* will convince them.

A tin of cockles can be quite pricy, because one tin contains many of these little shellfish. Because of the low demand in the United States, it can be tricky to get ahold of tinned cockles. You could purchase them online, a well-stocked fishmonger may sell them and many Spanish convenience stores also stock tins of *berberechos*. If you're in one of those stores, also get your hands on some fresh chorizo and Spanish rice. These go well with mussels and cockles to make a delicious *arroz*. Add a glass of white wine and enjoy these Spanish delicacies.

RAKING ON THE WADDEN SEA

With rhythmic movements, the photogenic Sjors rakes the seabed of the Engelsmanplaat, a sandbank between Ameland and Schiermonnikoog in the Wadden Sea. Sjors is hip-high in the fast-flowing water. A few more scrapes and it's back to the mother ship on a dinghy full of cockles. This raking technique ensures enough cockles are left for the oystercatchers. The fishermen have agreed to leave certain sandbanks in peace and to keep to yearly catch quotas. The MSC-certified cockle fishery in the Wadden Sea is a shining example of fishing while respecting the environment.

COQLADE

MAIN COURSE
SERVES 4

Mouclade, mussels in a creamy curry sauce, is a staple in French cuisine from the coastal town of La Rochelle. The French also enjoy their cockles with curry flavors, as in this *coqlade*.

2 heads garlic
9 oz/250 g cremini mushrooms
olive oil
1 oz/30 g butter
3 yellow onions, finely chopped
1 tbsp curry powder
1 glass of dry white wine
scant ½ cup/3½ fl oz/100 ml whipping cream
scant ½ cup/3½ fl oz/100 ml crème fraîche

5 saffron threads
generous ¾ cup/7 fl oz/200 ml chicken stock
2 red onions, chopped
2 tins of cockles (4¼ oz/120 g each), drained
1 baguette
sea salt and freshly ground black pepper

- Preheat the oven to 325°F/170°C.
- Wrap the heads of garlic in aluminum foil. Roast in the oven for 30 minutes, until the cloves have softened.
- Clean the mushrooms with a brush and cut into quarters.

- Heat a splash of olive oil in a frying pan. Fry the mushrooms over medium-high heat until golden brown on all sides.
- Remove the mushrooms from the pan, sprinkle with black pepper and set aside.
- Take the garlic out of the oven and leave to cool.
- Heat the butter in a large, heavy-bottomed pan and fry the finely chopped onions until they're translucent. Add the curry powder and leave to fry for 2 minutes over low heat.
- Deglaze by pouring in the white wine and boiling for a minute or so, stirring all the time.
- Cut the tops off the heads of garlic and squeeze out the cloves. Add the garlic to the curried onions.
- Add the cream, crème fraîche and saffron. Leave to simmer very gently for a few minutes. Do not allow the mixture to boil or the crème fraîche may separate.
- Add the chicken stock and a pinch of salt and leave to simmer for a few more minutes.
- Just before serving, add the mushrooms, red onions and cockles.
- Finally add a couple of decent cracks of black pepper and serve with slices of baguette.

ZUCCHINI AND FENNEL SOUP WITH COCKLES

STARTER
SERVES 4

olive oil
1 baby fennel bulb, chopped
2 zucchini, chopped
5 tbsp/3 fl oz/80 ml chicken
    stock
a few sprigs of flat-leaf parsley
2 tins of cockles in water
    (4¼ oz/120 g each),
    drained

a handful of chives, finely
    chopped
sea salt and freshly ground
    white pepper

- Heat a splash of olive oil in a frying pan over medium heat. Fry the fennel and zucchini for a few minutes, making sure you do not color the vegetables.
- Add the chicken stock, turn the heat down to low and simmer until the fennel is tender.
- Add the parsley sprigs, then purée the soup with an immersion blender. You want a chunky consistency.
- Season with salt and white pepper.
- Divide the soup among four bowls, then add the cockles to the bowls.
- Drizzle over a little more olive oil and garnish with the chives.

SPECIES	Herring
BINOMIAL NAME	*Clupea harengus*
FISHING METHODS	Pelagic trawling and purse seine
MSC CERTIFIED	Almost all herring from Denmark, the Netherlands and Scotland is certified (for more information on the MSC, see page 6)
TINNED OPTIONS	Herring in water, herring with tomato and basil, smoked herring in oil, smoked herring with pepper

HOW ABOUT A TIN OF HERRING WITH TOMATO AND BASIL? THAT'S HOW GOOD TINNED HERRING CAN BE.

HERRING

HERRING IS AVAILABLE BOTH PLAIN AND SMOKED, but it is probably smoked herring that is better known, and to many people in the United Kingdom, that means kippers, which are available both freshly smoked and in a tin. Because kippers were a Victorian favorite for breakfast and are an ingredient in the rice-based, Anglo-Indian dish kedgeree, some people may think of kippers as something quintessentially British. In fact, their popularity has waned considerably over the last century. When it comes to who actually originated kippers, opinions are divided. Conserving food by wood-smoking it is a technique a few thousand years old (if not more). The independent Food and Agriculture Organization of the United Nations is confident in naming the Dutch as the originators. The old-Dutch word *küppen* was initially used for lean salmon caught outside the season. An interesting kipper is the red herring, a red-brown smoked herring a couple sizes larger than our kipper.

THE UN'S FOOD AND AGRICULTURE ORGANIZATION

A real kipper is a split, cold-smoked herring. Split lengthwise, the filleted fish is connected from head to tail. The Dutch also have the *brado*, a halved kipper. The origin of brado is undisputed, and the locally famous Ouwehand family takes the credit. In the Netherlands, steamed buckling—a hot-smoked, steamed herring—is more popular than the kipper. Cold-smoked herring is called a bloater. The buckling and bloater don't end up in a tin, whereas the kipper often does. Tinned kipper is smoked in the same way as "fresh" kipper. For the tinned variety, the manufacturers can use lean herring, which is also used for pickled herring, called rollmops. This herring from the winter months is not fatty enough to be used as soused herring.

Many manufacturers offer MSC-certified herring, mostly derived from sustainable fisheries in Norway, Denmark or Scotland. These fisheries also fish for soused herring, as does the Dutch vessel *Hollandse Nieuwe*. They cast out ring nets and close them around a school of herring. The nets don't touch the bottom of the sea, which limits unwanted bycatch. Using this method, the fishermen take their responsibility for maintaining healthy fish stocks.

The major herring processors are found in Denmark and North Germany. Many herring fisheries nowadays meet the requirements set by the MSC. But that's not all. The factories, themselves also MSC-certified, produce delicious tinned fish filled with Scandinavian chefs' cleverly balanced sauces. How about a tin of herring with tomato and basil or a piri piri–mango sauce? These fish don't need much to go with them—a fresh slice of chunky bread at most. That's how good tinned herring can be.

CULINARY TINNED FISH FROM NORTH GERMANY

Frank Desler produces good herring in his cannery in north German Flensburg with tasty sauces—like tomato and basil—from Scandinavian chefs. He knows everything there is to know about herring and fully supports processing only sustainably caught fish. Preparing his fish, Frank pays close attention to the details. Too much heat can soften the herring too much, and Frank does not want herring paste. By parboiling the herring, the fillets soften without losing texture and flavor.

CAULIFLOWER PANNA COTTA WITH KIPPERS

MAIN COURSE
SERVES 4

1 small head cauliflower
olive oil
1 leek, white part only, finely chopped
dry white wine
scant ⅔ cup/5 fl oz/150 ml
    vegetable stock
1½ cups/12 fl oz/350 ml whipping
    cream
4 sheets of gelatin
1 tin of kippers in oil (6¾ oz/
    190 g), drained

1 tbsp white wine vinegar
10 capers, finely chopped
1 shallot, finely chopped
2 tbsp olive oil
1 tbsp hazelnut oil
1 tsp chopped flat-leaf parsley
salt and freshly ground
    white pepper

- Cut the cauliflower into large florets, then quarter half the cauliflower into smaller florets.
- Heat a dash of oil in a frying pan and braise the leek over low heat.
- Add the large cauliflower pieces and cook gently for 10 minutes or so.
- Deglaze with a splash of white wine and leave it to evaporate.
- Add the vegetable stock and season with salt and white pepper. Bring to a boil, then leave to simmer gently for about 10 minutes.
- Stir in the cream and leave the broth to settle for 15 minutes. Meanwhile, soak the gelatin sheets in a generous amount of cold water and grease four individual 2 in/5 cm ramekins with olive oil.
- When the cauliflower is cooked, purée the mixture, then press through a sieve. Squeeze the moisture from the gelatin and stir into the mixture until blended. Spoon into the ramekins and chill for about 4 hours.
- Take the panna cottas out of the fridge and turn out onto four plates. Arrange the kipper pieces around the panna cottas.
- Beat together the vinegar, capers, shallot and 2 tbsp olive oil.
- Heat the hazelnut oil in a frying pan. Fry the smaller cauliflower pieces quickly until lightly browned. Stir into the dressing.
- Pour the cauliflower dressing over the kippers and garnish with parsley.

KIPPER KEDGEREE

MAIN COURSE
SERVES 4

4 pappadams or crispy flatbread
    crackers
1⅔ cups/10½ oz/300 g
    basmati rice
3½ oz/100 g butter
4 tsp curry powder
¾ in/2 cm piece of fresh ginger,
    peeled and grated
2 yellow onions, finely chopped
3 tbsp chicken stock
3 eggs, hard-boiled and chopped
5 sprigs of cilantro, finely
    chopped

5 sprigs of flat-leaf parsley,
    finely chopped
1 lemon
2 tins of kippers in oil
    (6¾ oz/190 g each),
    drained
1 bunch of green onions,
    cut into rings
salt and freshly ground
    black pepper

- Prepare the pappadams according to the instructions on the package.
- Cook the rice according to the instructions on the package. The rice should be al dente, as it will be reheated later. Leave to cool.
- Melt the butter in a frying pan. Add the curry powder and grated ginger and fry for a minute.
- Add the onions and fry until translucent.
- Deglaze with the chicken stock and let the stock evaporate, stirring to mix in all the juices from the pan.
- Add the chopped eggs.
- Stir in the rice and heat through over low heat. Season the kedgeree with the cilantro, parsley, a squeeze of lemon juice, salt and pepper.
- Carefully stir the kipper pieces into the kedgeree.
- Serve the kedgeree sprinkled with broken pappadam pieces and green onions.

ACKNOWLEDGMENTS

THIS BOOK WAS CREATED WITH THE HELP OF MANY PEOPLE.

First, I want to thank Harry Visbeen. It's been a joyful and educational experience to cook with you, Harry! I'd also like to thank Franky Visbeen for the copious amounts of work you did in the kitchen. Thanks to Jos Schijff for making the kitchen of the ROC Mondriaan in The Hague available. And thanks to Jaap van Rijn for the wonderful photography.

I'd like to thank all the fishermen who catch the fish that end up in the Fish Tales tins: Zé Manel, Pat Pikus, Ali Mohamed, Poul Kaergaard, Frank Desler, Jack Webster, Mariano Di Scala and Sjors Schonewille.

For the welcome and guidance I received in Portugal I thank Maria Cristina, Sofia Brandão, Antonio Cunha, Sergio Real and Joao Coelho at the A Poveira S.A. cannery. For my trip to the Maldives my thanks go to John Burton and the other staff and fishermen at Horizon Fisheries Pvt. Ltd.

I would also like to thank everyone at Kosmos Publishers and especially Melanie Zwartjes who has fully supported this book from the start. Wouter Eertink, thank you for coordinating this process and Anne Wouters for coordinating the text. Tijs Koelmeijer, thanks for the beautiful design.

I thank my Fish Tales business partner Harm Jan van Dijk. It's going to be a great venture. Many thanks to Michiel Eliens for being a great help with the photography at Fish Tales. Thanks also to Julie van der Have. Thanks to Leo Hattenbach and Jaap Hoogendijk for believing in Fish Tales.

Thanks to Marcus Polman for his PR and marketing efforts and Judith Renard for the PR at Kosmos Publishers.

I want to thank Ivo van Kempen and everyone at Bagels & Beans, Rogier Soetens and the employees of Bakerstreet, Marc Dotinga and Marco Romeyn at Qizini and Roel Verwiel at KLM.

Last but not least, my thanks go to my darling Bernadien and my wonderful children Bo and Juul. Lots of love for my friends and family.

BART VAN OLPHEN

SARDINHAS EM TOMATE . SMALL SAR
SARDINHAS EM TOMATE · SARDINHAS INTOMAT
CEGO DO MAIO
CONSERVAS DA PÓVOA DE VARZIM

CEGO DO MAIO
CONSERVAS DA PÓVOA DE VARZIM
PONTE D. LUÍS
SARDINHAS PORTUGUESAS EM TOMATE PICANTE
PORTUGUESE SARDINES IN HOT TOMATO SAUCE

CEGO DO MAIO
CONSERVAS DA PÓVOA DE VARZIM
CAVALA.CAVALA.CAVALA.CAVALA
CAVALA.CAVALA.CAVALA.CAVALA.CAVALA
CAVALA
Mackerel Fillets in Olive Oil
FILETES EM AZEITE

CEGO DO MAIO
CONSERVAS DA PÓVOA DE VARZIM
SARDINES IN VEGETABLE OIL
PORTUGUESE SARDINES IN VEGETABLE
SARDINHAS PORTUGUESA EM ÓLEO VE

SARDIN
SE
E SEM
EM A
PIC

CEGO DO MAIO
CONSERVAS DA PÓVOA DE VARZIM
FILETS DE THON A L'HUILE D'OLIVE PIQUANTE
UNA FILLETES IN HOT OLIVE OIL. FILETES DE
EN ACEITE DE OLIVA PIC
ATUM
FILETES AZEITE PICANTE

CEGO DO MAIO
CONSERVAS DA PÓVOA DE VARZIM
PICANTE
SARDINHA
COM PICKLES

CEGO DO MAIO
CONSERVAS DA PÓVOA DE VARZIM
UNA FILLETES IN HOT OLIVE OIL WITH PICK
FILETES DE ATUM. FILETES DE ATUN
EN ACEITE DE OLIVA PICANTE CON PICKLES
ATUM
FILETES AZEITE PICANTE PICKLES

CEGO DO MAIO
CONSERVAS DA PÓVOA DE VARZIM
SAR DI NHA
EM TOMATE
Portuguese Sardines in Tomate Sauce

CEGO DO MAIO
CONSERVAS DA PÓVOA DE VARZIM
N

CEGO DO MAIO
CONSERVAS DA PÓVOA DE VARZIM
Sardinha sem Pele e sem Espinha em Tomate Picante

CEGO DO MAIO
CONSERVAS DA PÓVOA DE VARZIM
SAR DI NHA
EM TOMATE PICANTE
Portuguese Sardines in Hot Tomate Sauce

CEGO DO MAIO
CONSERVAS DA PÓVOA DE VARZIM
Sardinhas
Azeite & Alho
SARDINES IN OLIVE OIL AND GARLIC

CEGO DO MAIO
CONSERVAS DA PÓVOA DE VARZIM
SARDINES IN SPICED VEGETABLE OIL
SARDINHAS PORTUGUESAS EM ÓLEO VEGETAL PICANTE

MAQUEREAUX A L'HUILE D'OLIVE
OIL

CEGO DO MAIO
CONSERVAS DA PÓVOA DE VARZIM
Sardinha com AZEITE & LIMÃO
Portuguese Sardines in Olive Oil with Lemon

CEGO DO MAIO
CONSERVAS DA PÓVOA DE VARZIM
TORRE DOS CLÉRIGOS
SARDINHAS PORTUGUESAS EM AZEITE
PORTUGUESE SARDINES IN OLIVE OIL

CEGO DO MAIO
CONSERVAS DA PÓVOA DE VARZIM
8 A 12 SARDINHAS MIÚDAS "PETINGAS" EM TOMATE PICANTE
Small Sardines in Hot Tomato Sauce

CEGO DO MAIO
CONSERVAS DA PÓVOA DE VARZIM
SAR DI NHA
EM AZEITE
Portuguese Sardines in Olive Oil

Small